06

JUNIOR SURVIVAL LIBRARY

King of the beasts

THE LION

Caroline Brett

ANGLIA
Television Limited

Boxtree

Key to abbreviations

lb	pound
kg	kilogram
in	inch
ft	foot
yd	yard
cm	centimetre
m	metre
km	kilometre
sq mile	square mile
sq km	square kilometre
kph	kilometres per hour
mph	miles per hour

First published in 1990 by Boxtree Limited
Copyright © 1990 Survival Anglia Limited
Text copyright © 1990 Malcolm Penny

Front jacket photographs:
(Lion cub at 8 weeks old *and* Lion resting)
Survival Anglia/Jen & Des Bartlett
Back jacket photograph:
(A Lioness carrying her month-old cub)
Survival Anglia/Jen & Des Bartlett

Line drawings by Raymond Turvey

British Library Cataloguing in Publication Data
Brett, Caroline
    The lion.
    1. Lions.
    I. Title   II. Series
    599.74428

ISBN 1-85283-056-5

Edited by Miranda Smith
Designed by Groom & Pickerill
Typeset by Rowland Phototypesetting Limited
Bury St Edmunds, Suffolk

Printed and bound in Italy
by OFSA s.p.a.

for Boxtree Limited,
36 Tavistock Street,
London WC2E 7PB

Contents

Rulers of the plains

The lion is the most majestic **carnivore** in the world. It has the reputation of being fearless and immensely powerful. This is why it is often called the king of the beasts. Lions are very strong but they are not fearless. Joy Adamson, who wrote the book *Born Free*, found that the lion she and her husband looked after, Elsa, had paws that became damp when she was nervous. This is the lion's equivalent of breaking out in a sweat.

There are two kinds of lion alive today: the African lion, which is found mainly in central Africa, and the Asian lion, which only survives in one small forest in India. In this book we shall concentrate on the more familiar and common African lion.

Lions once had a much wider range. In prehistoric times, they lived all over Africa, as well as in India, Asia and Europe. Lion bones, together with the stone tools of prehistoric man, have been found in caves all over Europe. However, lions were killed by hunters because they were considered a threat to humans and their livestock. They were also hunted for sport. This and the increase in

The lion is the largest and strongest predator living on the African plains.

LION DISTRIBUTION

Range at end of ice age		Present day
Range in 1850		

Gir Forest (Present range of Asiatic lion)

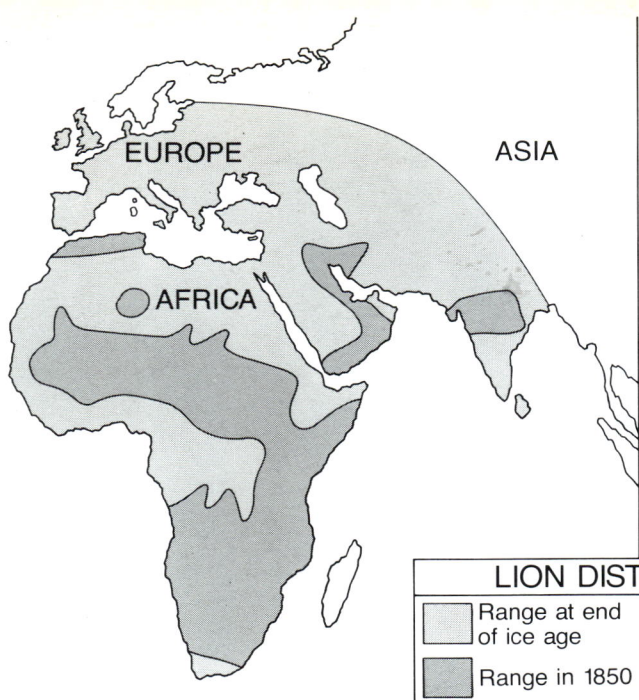

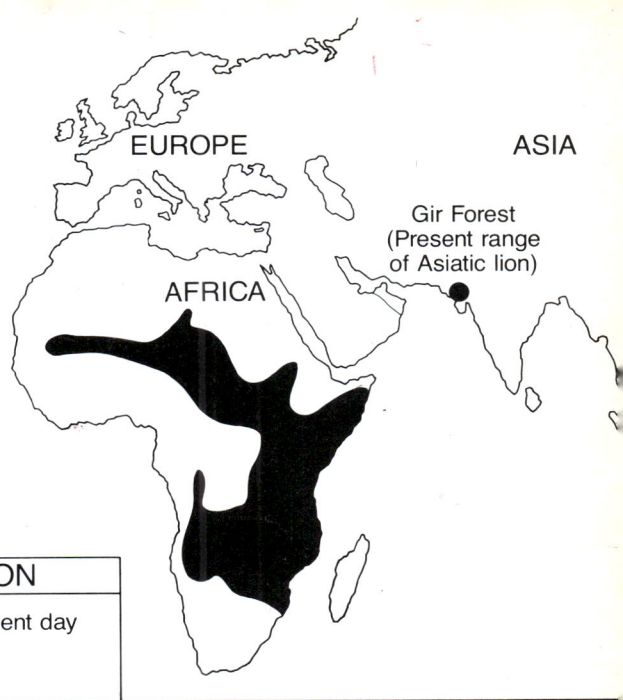

the human population caused the lions to retreat to remote, uninhabited regions.

By the end of the last century, lions were **extinct** everywhere except in India and Africa. Even in these countries they were hunted down and killed for sport or to safeguard live-stock. A magnificent black-maned lion, called the Cape lion, lived until recently in South Africa. But these superb animals were shot, trapped and poisoned by an ever-increasing number of farmers, until by the 1860s, the Cape lion was extinct.

Shaded from the mid-day heat, a lioness dozes comfortably in the branches of a tree.

Tree-climbing lions

Lions do not usually climb trees, but there are always exceptions to the general rule. Several **prides** in the Queen Elizabeth Park in Uganda, and others in Manyara Game Reserve in Kenya, often climb into their favourite tree during the heat of the day. They probably do this to catch any breeze and to escape from biting flies. There seem to be obvious advantages, so why do not other lions follow their example? No one really knows the answer. It may be because there are no suitable trees with wide, spreading branches in other parts of Africa. Whatever the reason, these prides have become a star attraction and people travel miles to photograph them. Tourist hotels even advertise special excursions to see the famous tree-climbing lions.

5

Asian lions

Asian lions are closely related to African lions, but there are differences, the biggest of which is that most Asian lions have a smaller mane. Asian lions are stockier in build and have a thicker coat than African lions. They also have a longer tail tassel, a more pronounced belly fringe, and hairy elbows.

Asian lions are very rare today, but 130 years ago they were common in northern India. They live in open, dry, scrub country. Unlike African lions, which hunt mainly at night, Asian lions are most active during the day. This has made them easy **prey** for hunters, especially sportsmen with guns.

Disgruntled villagers, whose cattle had been killed by lions, also poisoned them. By the early 1900s there were fewer than 20 left. Only then was the Asian lion officially declared a protected animal. These last few animals lived in the Gir Forest Reserve in north-west India and today there are over 200 in here.

Opposite *Asian lions are one of the rarest animals in India.*

Below left *Asian lions often kill domestic water buffalo because there are so few of their natural prey in India.*

Yet even here the lions are seriously threatened. More than 7,000 humans and approximately 57,000 domestic animals use the forest. The cattle and water buffalo compete for food together with the lion's natural prey, such as deer. The numbers of deer and wild pig living in the Gir Forest have declined rapidly in recent years and as a result the lions have resorted to taking and eating the domestic stock. They kill between 10 and 20 cattle or water buffalo a day.

The local people seem content to accept these losses of livestock as part of the price they must pay for the privilege of grazing the government-owned forest. But there are too many cattle and water buffalo, and they are slowly eating the vegetation in the forest and trampling it down. If their numbers are not drastically reduced, scientists estimate that the forest will be destroyed in the next 20 years. And if the Gir Forest is destroyed, so too will be the last Asian lions.

King of the beasts

The king of the beasts, the male lion, is the largest predator in Africa. A mature beast can weigh 250 kg (550 lb) – which is three times as much as a man – measure 320 cm (10 ft 6 ins) from nose to tail, and stand 120 cm (4 ft) high.

The main role of a male is to defend the females, the cubs, and their **territory** from rival males. At the approach of an intruder, the resident males try to make themselves look as big and fearsome as possible. They stand on their toes, throw out their chests, tense all their muscles and raise their manes. Confrontations between rival males are usually settled without a fight. The smaller animals back off before this happens.

Lions can live to be 30 years old in captivity, but they rarely reach anything like that age in the wild. Young males are driven from their pride when they are between two and three years old by the resident adult males. They usually leave with other youngsters, often their brothers and cousins. The **bachelors** wander over the plains in small groups, hunting as a team for the next year or two. During this period, they become a close-knit group and will probably stay together for life.

When the young lions are fully grown, they start looking for a pride of their own. They will challenge and fight with weaker or ageing males and try to take over a pride. If they gain control, they can be leaders for as little as 18 months or as long as ten years, depending on how successful they are at driving off other unattached males wandering the plains in search of mates.

Opposite *A moth probes for moisture in a sleeping lion's eye.*

Left *The main role of the males is to protect the pride from other marauding males.*

The lion's mane

The larger male lions are usually the dominant ones. But there are limits; the larger a lion gets, the slower and more cumbersome he becomes, and the more food he needs. A very big lion is likely to die of starvation. To give an appearance of great size without the drawbacks of increased weight, male lions **evolved** a huge **mane**.

Manes also serve as shields. When two males of equal size and strength meet, they sometimes fight. Then, the thick hair of their manes protects them, particularly the vulnerable throat area, from another lion's teeth and claws.

Queen of the beasts

Lionesses are much smaller than their mates. They do not need to fight to stay in their pride, and so have no need to be big or grow a mane. They are often called the queen of the beasts because they run the family and provide for it. Since they are of smaller build than the males, they are more agile and can run faster. As a result, the lionesses catch almost all of the pride's food.

Female lions live much longer than males in the wild because they usually stay with their family group for life. If they do not die of old age or starvation, **parasites** like ticks seem to be the biggest killer.

Lionesses start breeding when they are two to three years old. They can produce young at any time of year, although several females in the pride may give birth in the same month. They have a short pregnancy of three and a half months, compared with nine for humans. When the cubs are born, they are blind and completely dependent on their mother.

Lionesses usually give birth to two or three cubs in a sheltered place. This is often a cave or gully, where the cubs are protected from hyenas, leopards or even other lions, which might eat them. The cubs' eyes open after six days, but their mother will not introduce them to the rest of the pride until they are four to eight weeks old.

The cubs' spotted coats help to keep them concealed from sharp-eyed **predators**. If a female suspects that her lair has been discovered, she will carry the cubs, one by one, to a new, safer home. Predators are not the only danger the cubs have to face. In the rainy season their hideaway may become flooded and the young lions can drown, or become soaked to the skin and die of exposure.

Opposite *A lioness scans the plains for prey. It is the females which do most of the hunting.*

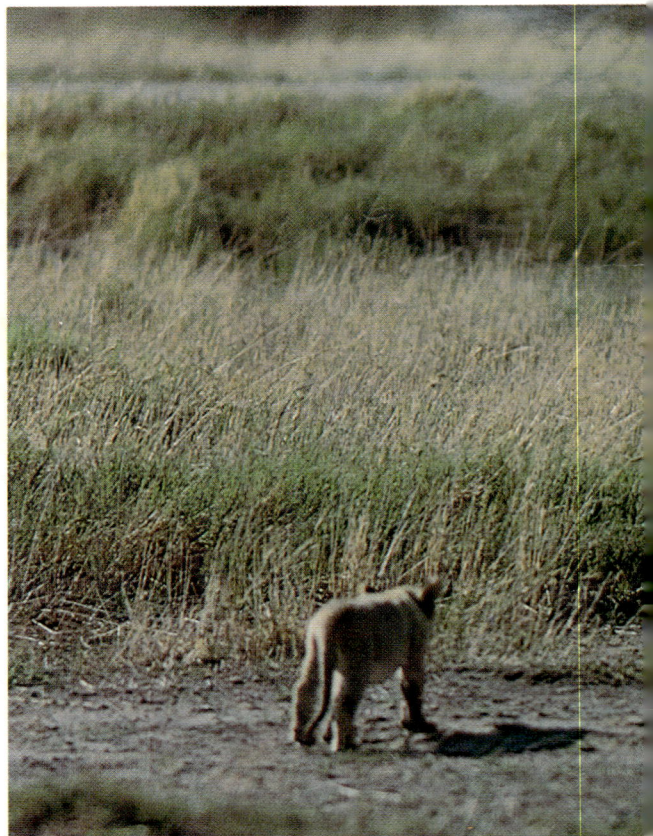

Left *Lionesses help each other rear young. This female is taking all the cubs in her pride for a drink.*

The pride

The lion is the only cat which lives in large groups. These prides contain up to 30 individuals. There are usually four to 12 adult females, their offspring, and two to four adult males in each pride. Prides of more than 50 animals have been known, but are very rare.

The pride males are outsiders who join a group of females. The lionesses are all born into the pride and form an association of mothers, daughters, grandmothers and aunts, all with their own offspring. The females inherit the territory. By living in a large group they can defend and pass this territory on to their daughters.

Lionesses will nurse each other's young. Cubs from four different mothers have been seen suckling at the same time from one

The lion is the most social of all cats. They live together peacefully in groups called prides.

Cubs of the same sex which grow up together, often remain friends for life.

Killing Cubs

Male lions are gentle and patient fathers to their own offspring and will tolerate having their manes and tails pulled for hours. But when a new group of males takes over a pride, they often kill all the young cubs. This is called **infanticide**. It may seem cruel and aggressive, but the males have good reason. Within two or three years they would probably be chased away in turn and lose the females so, during that time, they must try to have cubs of their own. If a lioness already has young cubs, it will be two years before she will have more. The new males cannot afford to spend two years raising another male's offspring. If they kill the cubs, the females can have a new litter within five months and then the new males will have heirs.

Lions are very patient with their offspring. Cubs are allowed to climb all over a sleeping adult.

lioness. This has its advantages. If one lioness dies, her cubs will not necessarily die as well, as her relatives will continue to care for them. Each lioness may also produce different **antibodies** in her milk, so that suckling from several females may give the cubs a greater **immunity** to disease.

The males do not fight over the females, partly because they have known each other from birth, but also because they need to join forces in order to drive off rival males. Instead, the first male to find a female in breeding condition is accepted as being dominant over the others.

The home range

African lions live in a variety of **habitats**. They are found mainly in the rich grasslands of East Africa, but they also live in scrub-country, known as the **bush**, and even in the sands of the Kalahari Desert.

A pride can range over an area of between 20 and 400 sq km (eight to 155 sq miles). The territory size depends on the number of lions in the pride and the amount of prey available. The scarcer the prey, the further afield the lions have to hunt. Large ranges may overlap with neighbouring lions, although each pride has a central area which they regard as their own.

All pride members, except the small cubs, patrol their **boundaries**. At regular intervals, the males spray prominent landmarks, like bushes and boulders, with urine. This leaves a strong smell that lingers for days. For any

A lion responds to the scent of an intruding male or a receptive female by curling back his lips.

The lion's roar

Lions roar to communicate with other lions. Both sexes roar, often in unison. Roaring warns rival prides to keep their distance. The sound can be heard 8 km (5 miles) away on a still night and any lions within earshot will usually roar back. Lions sometimes use a muffled roar when they are patrolling their territory or during a hunt to keep in touch with other members of their pride.

Like domestic cats, lions purr when they are contented and growl when they are angry.

Above *Roaring lions advertise their presence in order to avoid encounters with neighbours.*

strange lions, the message is clear – stay away, the territory is occupied. Any pride trespassing on its neighbour's territory can expect a show-down. Such displays of strength happen quite often, as the prides try to enlarge their range at their neighbour's expense.

Below *A male sprays urine on a large tuft of grass in order to scent-mark its territory.*

Lion food

Above *When herds of wildebeest migrate through a pride's territory, the lions have more than enough to eat.*

The lion's favourite prey is zebra and large antelopes, like wildebeest. There are millions of wildebeest in Africa; sometimes the whole landscape can appear to be alive with them. The herds wander across the plains, following the rains and the new grass on which they feed.

Wildebeest and zebra are **migratory** animals, which means they are constantly on the move. They travel thousands of miles every year in their continual search for food. Lions are territorial and stay in one place for most of their lives. When the great herds move into their range, the lions have an abundant source of food. However, when the zebra and antelopes move on to fresh pastures, the lions can go hungry.

The food a lion eats depends on where it lives, the prey found in its range and how many mouths there are to feed. When there are no zebra or wildebeest to hunt, lions will eat a great variety of prey. They have been seen to tackle baby elephants and rhinos, as well as crocodiles, hippos, **rodents**, birds, tortoises and prickly porcupines. Some even take ostrich eggs. Although they are basically meat-eaters, they will eat fruit, seeds, locusts, termites and groundnuts if other food is scarce and they are very hungry.

Bachelor males find it hard to hunt because they are large and easy to see. They sometimes kill large, lumbering buffalo. Warthogs are a

Left *The zebra is one of the lion's favourite prey animals.*

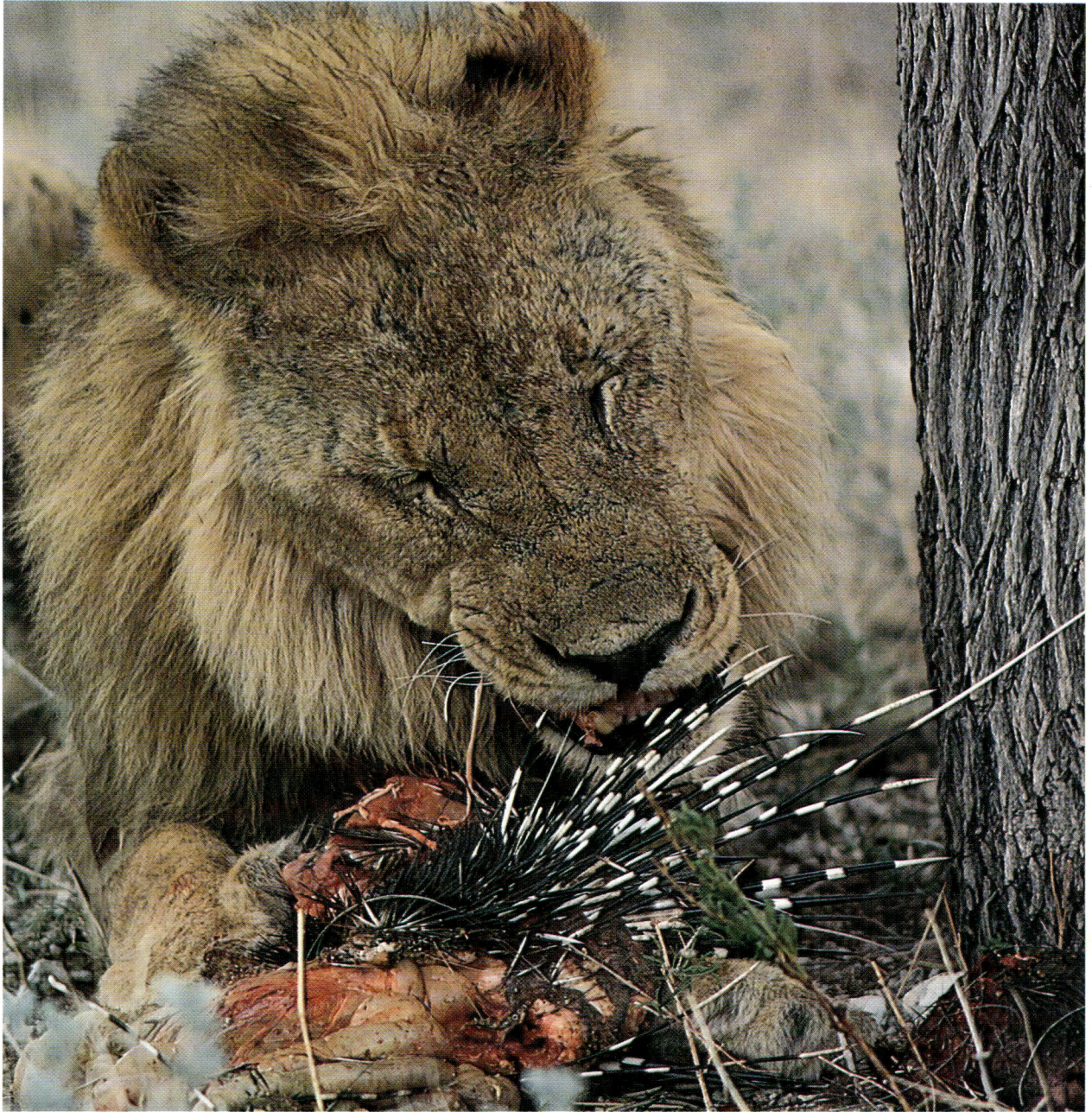

A lion will eat anything it can catch, even porcupines, if it is hungry enough.

favourite prey and bachelors have been seen patiently waiting and watching by a bog hole for hours, and even digging them out if they do not appear.

Lions get their vitamins from the **entrails** of their prey. They will usually eat the guts first in order to get these essential ingredients in their diet. Then, starting from the hindquarters, they eat their way upwards towards the head. Within 15 minutes of the lion making a small kill, all that is left of the prey, apart from one or two bones, are a few blood stains in the grass.

The hunt

At dusk, the lions stretch themselves, yawn and prepare for a night's work. When a pride of lions goes after big game, the females always take the lead. The males usually tag along behind the females because they are lazy and their manes can make them conspicuous.

As they near the herds of antelope and zebra, the lionesses fan out. The idea is to encircle the prey and cut off any potential escape routes. Although lions can reach speeds of 58 kph (36 mph) their prey can dash away at 80 kph (50 mph). So the lionesses must approach with stealth and try to get within 30 m (100 ft) of the prey. From this distance the predator can charge the herds and either grab a fleeing animal or trip one up before it has time to outrun its enemies.

Surprisingly, lions do not take wind direction into account during a hunt, despite the fact that they are more successful when stalking upwind. It seems that this is a tactic which lions have never learned. Only about one in four charges is successful, usually because the prey get wind of the pride before they have a chance to close in. But once it has been knocked down, a victim has little chance. Large animals are suffocated either by a bite to the throat or by clamping their mouth and nose shut so that they cannot breathe.

A lioness is perfectly camouflaged against a background of dry grasses.

Settling into a good meal, four lionesses share a wildebeest carcass.

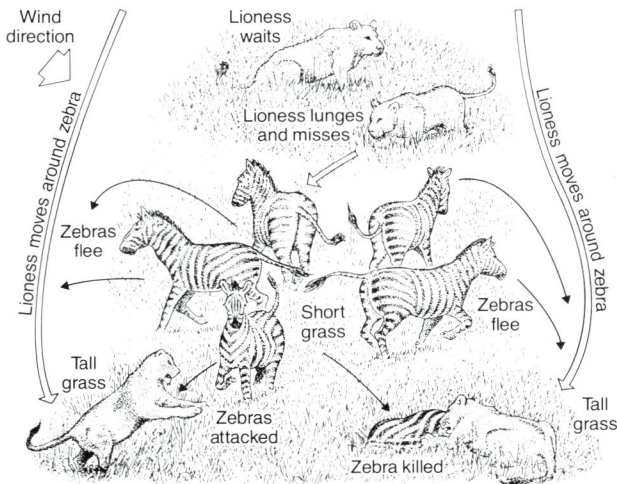

Co-operation works for the lionesses in this hunt. Two lions circle the herds and take up crouching positions about 90 m (100 yds) apart. When the zebra get wind of the rest of the pride, they stampede towards the lions lying in wait. Caught in the ambush, the zebra are easy prey.

Ambush

To set up an ambush requires team work. By co-operating with each other, lionesses can use the advantage of surprise. Two or three females slowly circle round the herds, keeping at a distance in order not to alarm their prey. They have a great talent for concealment. Their tawny coats blend in perfectly with dry grass and they take advantage of the smallest cover, flattening themselves so close to the ground that they seem part of it. At the far side of the herds, they lie in wait hidden in the long grass. Eventually, one member of the pride is spotted and she drives the unsuspecting prey straight into the jaws of her waiting companions.

The lion's share

Adult males rarely take part in the kill. They do not expend much effort during the chase, neither do they risk being kicked by a struggling zebra. Yet they are almost always the first to eat. As soon as the prey is down, the males muscle their way in and eat their fill.

It is easy to see where the expression 'the lion's share' came from! The males' greater size gives them a huge advantage. They can crowd out the females and cubs, and even take

The males feast first, even though the actual kill was made by the lionesses.

possession of the entire kill, if it is a small antelope or warthog.

When prey is scarce, there is a great deal of snarling and squabbling over the kill, as each member of the pride struggles to get its share. After the males, the females are next in line, with the cubs last of all. When food runs low, the cubs suffer first and many will die. Even their mother will prevent them from eating, if she is very hungry. As many as 80 per cent of cubs die before they are two years old, but if they all survived, Africa would soon become overrun with lions.

The cubs are always the last to eat. When prey is scarce, they are the ones who go short.

Adult males need about 7 kg (16 lb) of meat a day and lionesses about 5 kg (11 lb). But lions in the wild do not eat regular meals. They usually kill every two or three days and then gorge themselves. They can pack away 23 kg (50 lb) of meat at one meal. If a lion is three times as big as a human, that is the equivalent of a man eating 17 large steaks for dinner.

After a feast, the pride retires to the shade of a tree, where they sprawl and rest for up to four days while they digest their huge meal.

Lions spend as much as 20 hours a day sleeping or resting.

Midnight prowlers

When lions bring down an animal, the noise and commotion at the scene of the kill quickly attracts the attention of the hangers-on or **scavengers**. Jackals and hyenas are often seen around a pride of lions. They wait patiently for the lions to finish their meal and then pick up the scraps. They will also dart in and grab a mouthful of meat if the opportunity arises, much to the annoyance of the lions.

Although jackals and hyenas will eat any food they find lying about, both species are also expert hunters. They earned their reputation as scavengers because, until recently, they were only observed during the day. When they were studied at night, it was dis-

covered that hyenas hunt in packs and kill zebra and antelopes themselves.

On some African game reserves, 80 per cent of the food eaten by hyenas consists of animals they have killed. Jackals, too, catch much of their own food. Being agile and able to run fast, they are clever at catching young antelopes, mice, rats, lizards and other small creatures. Neither animal is the coward it was once thought to be. Hyenas will attempt to defend

Below *Spotted hyenas are also called 'laughing hyenas' because of their loud cackling call.*

Opposite *Jackals are efficient hunters.*

The scavenging lion

A pride of lions feeding on a kill in broad daylight is very likely to have stolen its meal from another predator. If the lions hear or see another hunter bring down an animal, they will move in, hoping that their strength and ferocity will drive off the rightful owners. They usually succeed! Lions living on the Serengeti plains scavenge more than half of their food.

their prey from all rivals and jackals will bark sharply at larger carnivores in protest. Jackals have even been seen to chase off a scavenging hyena. This is a brave act because lions, leopards and hyenas sometimes kill jackals.

Vultures obtain all their food by scavenging, but they irritate lions less than the other hangers-on because they are active during the day. Lions hunt mainly at night, but vultures have to wait until the sun heats up the ground and warm air starts to rise, before they can get airborne.

The big five

There are five large carnivores living on the African plains – the lion, the leopard, the cheetah, the hyena and the African hunting dog.

The lion's greatest competitor is the hyena. Both animals hunt at night and in large groups. They go after the same prey, steal food from one another and occasionally even kill each other.

Prowling in packs, hyenas are cunning and fierce killers. Like lions, their chief prey are zebra and wildebeest, but they use a different hunting technique. While lions lie in wait and kill any animal which comes within reach, hyenas study the herds before attacking. They select an animal which appears weaker or slower than the rest and then chase it.

African hunting dogs or wild dogs are probably the most efficient killers on the plains. Like hyenas, they also work in packs, select the old and the weak, and hunt wildebeest and zebra. Since wild dogs hunt mainly during the day, they do not compete with lions in the same way as hyenas.

Few animals can out-distance wild dogs, because they can run tirelessly for miles, at a maximum speed of 64 kph (40 mph). They will chase an animal until it is exhausted. If a wildebeest tries to stand and fight, its fate is soon sealed. With as many as 20 animals on its

The African hunting dog is an endangered animal. There may only be 10,000 left in the world.

heels, it is not long before one member of the pack can creep up unnoticed from behind and grab a back leg. Once one dog has a grip, the others rush in, and the wildebeest goes down in a confusion of thrashing legs and snapping jaws.

Leopards are large and powerful cats, but they hunt alone. They are unable to tackle large game by themselves, so do not compete with lions for their favourite prey. Leopards stalk small antelopes and only make a final attack when they are a few metres away. They often drag their kill up into a tree, to keep them out of the reach of scavenging lions and hyenas.

Cheetahs can reach speeds of 96 kph (60 mph), which makes them the fastest animals on four legs. They are smaller than lions and sprint after their prey, trying to run them down. They also hunt during the day and eat gazelle, impala and wildebeest calves, so they pose no great threat to the resident pride of lions.

A cheetah sits on top of a termite mound for a better view of its surroundings.

Waterhole

Much of the open country in Africa where lions live turns into parched semi-desert in the dry season. During these months, the sun is very hot and no rain falls. The zebra and wildebeest move far away to where water is always available. But the lions remain. When the rivers dry up, the only places to find a drink are a few isolated waterholes. Sooner or later, wildlife from miles around congregates at these. Some animals come to bathe, most to drink, but the lions also come to hunt.

Lions drink regularly if water is available, but they can go for days without drinking. In desert areas, lions obtain liquid from the stomachs of their prey. They also pull up roots and chew them for their moisture. The famous explorer, Livingstone even recorded Kalahari lions eating wild melons for their juices.

Although lions usually hunt at night, at a waterhole they are also active during the day. This is because their prey leave the waterhole at sunset for the comparative safety of the open plains. Only in broad daylight, when they can see all around them, do prey animals risk

Above *Lions drink every day when possible but they can go for several days without water.*

Opposite *A pride of lions lines up at the edge of a waterhole, waiting for prey coming to drink under the cover of darkness.*

quenching their thirst. Impala and gazelle approach a waterhole very cautiously, they can sense danger. But eventually their need to drink overrides their sense of fear. The lions wait patiently out of sight until the herds have their heads down. Only then, when their prey are at a disadvantage, do they launch an attack.

The height of the dry season is an easy time for lions because their prey are all concentrated in one place. At the start of the wet season the waterholes cease to be the centre of activity. When the storm clouds break and the rain falls, there is both food and water out on the plains. As the game moves away from the permanent sources of water, the lions follow them. After several downpours, the waterhole will be fuller, and the water a lot fresher, but there will not be an animal in sight.

Lion and man

Man has always held the lion in great awe. The Romans imported more than 50,000 lions from Africa and Asia, put them into pits and threw undesirables to them. This practice continued in Europe into medieval times.

The myth that lions have supernatural powers still survives in Africa today. Some tribes believe that by eating or wearing parts of a lion, they can revive lost powers, cure illnesses and gain immunity from death. Others believe that a lion's blood sprinkled on a cancer will cure it. Lion fat is recommended as a treatment for various problems including swollen glands and dislocated bones.

The powerful image of the lion has drawn hunters from all over the world who believe they are showing their courage and prowess by shooting one. In the past, sportsmen regularly killed up to a dozen lions per hunting trip. In India, a Mogul emperor of the seventeenth century is reputed to have hunted lions with an army of 100,000 men. Lions may be very powerful, but they are no match for a man armed with a gun.

Today, hunting is controlled, but lions continue to attract thousands of tourists to Africa. Fortunately the only trophy these people are after is a snapshot for the family album.

Man-hunter

Some lions become man-eaters in the wild. These are often old or wounded animals which are unable to kill their usual prey. If the number of prey animals drops drastically because of hunting, over-grazing or drought, starving lions will kill people. Towards the end of the last century, two apparently healthy lions preyed regularly on the labourers working on the Uganda–Kenya railway. They killed more than 30 men in just over a year and they terrorised the labour force to such an extent that construction work was halted until the lions had been shot.

Man-eater. It is usually only old, sick or starving lions which resort to killing people.

A more serious threat to the survival of this superb animal comes from the fact that the game on which the lions feed needs large areas of land for grazing. Unfortunately this is a resource which is fast disappearing. When the game has gone, the lions either face starvation or resort to killing domestic stock. When this happens, they are often shot by angry farmers.

A lion, safe in its natural habitat in a Rhodesian National Park.

Lions are able to breed successfully in zoos, so they are unlikely to become extinct. But a caged lion cannot be compared with the magnificent king of the beasts which roams freely over the plains of Africa.

29

Glossary

Antibody A defensive substance produced in the body of an animal in response to a foreign body such as a parasite.

Bachelor A male which is unattached to a female.

Boundary The outer limits of a territory.

Bush Uncultivated and uninhabited land in countries such as Africa.

Carnivore An animal which eats flesh.

Entrails An animal's intestines.

Evolution The slow process by which animals change over many generations, to adapt to their environment.

Extinct Animal species that have died out.

Habitat An area in which an animal normally lives.

Immunity The ability to resist illness or infection.

Infanticide The killing of offspring by the male lions.

Mane The long hair along the top and sides of the head of a lion.

Migratory Regularly travelling long distances between two places, usually along a particular route.

Parasite An animal which feeds on another animal.

Predator An animal that hunts and kills other animals for food.

Prey Animals that are hunted and killed by other animals.

Pride A group of lions.

Rodent A group of small mammals, such as squirrels, rats and mice.

Scavenger An animal which feeds on rubbish and the remains of dead animals.

Territory An area which an animal regards as its own, where it feeds and breeds, and which it defends against others.

About the author

Caroline Brett has a B.Sc. Hons degree in Zoology from Bristol University. After travelling through North, Central and South America she joined Radio Avonside (now Great Western Radio). Caroline now works for Survival Anglia as a writer and producer of natural history documentaries for the long-running Survival series and has also made programmes for Anglia Television's children's series ANIMALS IN ACTION.

Index

The entries in **bold** are illustrations.

Picture Acknowledgements

The publishers would like to thank the
Survival Anglia picture library
and the following photographers for the use
of photographs on the pages listed:

R. L. Matthews 4; Bruce Davidson 5, 14; Joanna Van Gruisen 7; Dieter & Mary Plage 6, 29; Purdy & Matthews 8, 21; Jen & Des Bartlett 9, 10, 11, 16, 17, 18, 20, 26, 27; Bob Campbell 12, 19, 22, 23; J. M. Pearson 24; Alan Root 25.